WOMEN BUSI
OF .....
U.S. HEALTH CARE INDUSTRY FOUNDATION™
WWW.WOMENLEADINGHEALTHCARE.ORG
PROMOTING *HORIZONTAL ADVANCEMENT*™

MW00653292

ADVANCING
Women IN BUSINESS

10 BEST PRACTICES

With a Special Focus on
Board Placement

Lynn Shapiro Snyder

Created in collaboration with

EPSTEIN BECKER & GREEN P.C.
THOUGHT LEADERS IN
HEALTH LAW®

WWW.EBGLAW.COM

Published by Women Business Leaders of the U.S. Health Care Industry Foundation, 1227 25th Street NW, Washington, DC 20037, **www.womenleadinghealthcare.org**.

Snyder, Lynn Shapiro.

Advancing Women in Business: 10 Best Practices

ISBN-10: 0-9797557-1-9
ISBN-13: 978-0-9797557-1-2

Printed in the United States of America, Washington, D.C.
First Edition

TABLE OF CONTENTS

PART I: Vertical and Horizontal Advancement™

Introduction: The Ten Best Practices for Advancing Women in Business 9

Chapter 1: Self-Promoting 11

Chapter 2: Cultivating Business Relationships................ 15

Chapter 3: Being Proactive about Advancement 19

Chapter 4: Making your Objectives Known 21

Chapter 5: Delegating 23

Chapter 6: Striking a Work/Life Balance 27

Chapter 7: Informal Networking 31

Chapter 8: Passing Opportunities Along.......................... 35

Chapter 9: Learning from Challenges.............................. 39

Chapter 10: Focusing on Communication Styles.............. 43

continues

PART II: Breaking the Glass Boardroom Door

PREFACE

My name is Lynn Shapiro Snyder. I currently practice health care and life sciences law in Washington, D.C. for Epstein Becker & Green, P.C. I have been at my firm since 1979. My areas of expertise are in Medicare, Medicaid, and Compliance matters. However, those are not the subjects that I will be covering in this book.

I am not just a health care and life sciences lawyer. I also am senior management in my law firm. Indeed, I am a senior attorney at one of the nation's AMLAW 200 law firms, a firm that also happens to have one of the nation's largest health care and life sciences practices (with over 125 lawyers working full time on health care and life sciences clients).

Do you think that law school prepared me for my advancement and management duties at the law firm? Not really. How about my undergraduate work? It was in economics—actually with a concentration in health economics—but that has not really helped me with my advancement and management duties. Recognizing this unmet need, I read self-help books, and I watched how others have advanced in business and managed others. I also reached out to people outside my law firm and discovered other senior executive women in the health care industry with similar unmet needs. They also had worked diligently over the last twenty-five to thirty years and were now the "boss" or almost the "boss." How did they achieve their senior executive status and what were they doing to manage others effectively and continue to advance their careers?

Often, in the health care industry, health professionals are promoted to management like I was at my law firm. Nurses and physicians excel in their professions and then are rewarded with management duties. Yet many of us could use some help in managing our businesses and advancing our careers.

In that regard, I started an organization in 2001 called the Women Business Leaders of the U.S. Health Care Industry Foundation™ (WBL, at www.womenleadinghealthcare.org). WBL currently includes among its Foundation Associates over 1,700 senior executive women and women board members from all over the world who are involved in all sectors of the U.S. health care and life sciences industry—manufacturers, payers, providers of all types, and health care industry service providers.

WBL's mission is twofold:

First, WBL's mission is to help senior executive women and women board members improve their health care businesses. We do this by creating meaningful business networking opportunities; these women should never have a "cold" call in the U.S. health care industry.

Second, WBL's mission is to help senior executive women continue to grow professionally *even after* they are in senior management. We do this by presenting educational programs on executive MBA topics, as well as by helping many WBL Foundation Associates serve on corporate for profit boards. Serving on a corporate for profit board is an excellent way for a senior manager to continue to grow professionally.

Many WBL Foundation Associates already have successfully advanced to senior management status. This often is called "vertical advancement" in one's career—it refers to advancing one's status through promotions or job changes.

However, once you are the boss (or almost the boss) how do you continue to grow professionally? In that context, I have coined the phrase "Horizontal Advancement™" to focus on community or corporate board service as an opportunity for senior executives to continue to grow professionally and give back by helping others run their companies or organizations. In my own career, for example, I currently serve as a member of the board of a mutual insurance company in addition to being on the board of my law firm.

My own personal experiences—at my firm and through my corporate board service—along with my interaction with WBL Foundation Associates, has given me many insights in connection with both vertical and Horizontal Advancement™. WBL women have shared their thoughts and served as collective mentors. After all, who mentors the mentors? We mentor each other. This book includes some of the key lessons I have learned.

I hope this information helps you achieve your business and professional goals.

Lynn Shapiro Snyder

January 2008

PART I

Vertical and Horizontal Advancement™

VERTICAL ADVANCEMENT:
Advancing in one's career to achieve senior management status, such as through promotions or job changes.

HORIZONTAL ADVANCEMENT™:
Advancement of a senior executive's career through means other than promotions or job changes—such as through corporate board service or community service.

PART I ◆ INTRODUCTION

The Ten Best Practices for Advancing Women in Business

During the first national WBL Foundation Summit on March 6-8, 2002, we convened approximately 100 successful senior executive women from the U.S. health care industry— for the first time. During the Summit, we asked one compelling question:

> *What were some of the best practices you used to become successful in your career?*

We aggregated and prioritized the responses to create the following "Top Ten" list of Best Practices.

Ten Best Practices for Advancing Women in Business

1. Find your style and self-promote. Self-promotion not only is appropriate, but expected.

2. Invest time in cultivating business relationships—take some action at least once a week. Do not merely be a "doer."

3. Be proactive about your advancement. Take deliberate steps toward your goals.

4. Make your business and professional objectives known to others, directly or indirectly.

5. Be comfortable with delegating and surround yourself with excellent talent.

6. Find your work/life balance and help others do the same. Work/life balance is good for business.

continues

7. Create your own meeting. Informal networking can be just as effective as formal networking. You do not need to wait for meetings or retreats to network with others relevant to your business.

8. When you are not interested in an opportunity, make recommendations and pass the information along. Every opportunity that comes your way is an opportunity for someone.

9. Learn from challenges. Failures are just challenges. You can learn a lot from challenges.

10. Focus on communication styles. Become knowledgeable about differences in communication styles. Know your audience and communicate in their style.

In Part I, I will discuss each of these Advancement Best Practices in a detailed chapter. You will notice that my examples are from the health care industry. Nevertheless, they translate easily to other industries. In any event, I hope that Part I of this book demonstrates for you, in some detail, how you can benefit from this list.

PART I ◆ CHAPTER 1

Self-Promoting

Find your style and self-promote.
Self-promotion not only is appropriate, but expected.

When was the last time you told someone outside your family that you had achieved a milestone in the workplace? Consider the following hypothetical. Does it sound familiar?

Two executives in an integrated health care delivery system have equal seniority. The system includes a few hospitals, some physician practices, and some ancillary services in a major metropolitan area. One of the executives, Samantha Smith, achieved a successful milestone in the workplace by getting a small rural hospital about one hour from the "mother ship" hospital to become an affiliate of the system. It is the first time the system has been able to penetrate this new geographic area. This affiliation was one of the key goals of this system's five-year strategic plan.

The second executive, Jane Jones, also recently achieved a successful milestone in the workplace by establishing a new division within the mother ship hospital for conducting clinical trial research for the development of new drugs and devices. This required recruiting the right personnel, establishing the right policies and procedures, and marketing to manufacturers to develop this new income stream. This new division also was one of the key goals of the system's five-year strategic plan.

Samantha Smith makes it a point to get on the calendar of her Board's Chairperson for a private lunch. During the lunch, Samantha walks the Chair through how Samantha achieved the goal of attracting the rural hospital to join the system. Samantha also asks to present at the upcoming System's Board

Retreat so that the board can hear firsthand about this wonderful accomplishment.

Jane Jones is very busy actually running the division she created until she recruits the new person to take over those duties. Jane has been sending written reports to the Board's Chairperson to apprise the board of her achievements. Jane is not going to attend the upcoming Board Retreat because, as a result of her recent late nights doing her own job and the new division job, she would prefer to use the weekend to rest.

What is wrong with this picture? In this chapter, we are focusing on self-promotion. Why are some women reluctant or otherwise not focused on self-promotion in the workplace? Is there something in a woman's upbringing that stifles these statements? Do women think it is bragging? Well, we need to get over that! (In Part I, Chapter 5, we will focus on the need to delegate effectively to advance in business.)

On the other hand, why are most men comfortable and, to a great extent, strategic in their self-promotion activities? Self-promotion appears to come to many men so naturally. Men appear to understand that businesses are hierarchical and that the personal objective is to climb up the business mountain. An October 2007 study published by McKinsey & Company confirmed through research that "one of the keys to success lies in the ability to promote oneself and to be assertive about one's performance and ambitions" – and that the women who were successful in business showed a great degree of adaptation to this "masculine model of upward mobility."[1]

---

[1]   Devillard, Sandrine, McKinsey & Company, *Women Matter*, 8 (2007), available at http://www.mckinsey.com/careers/women/ makingadifference/socialsectorimpact/womenmatter/.

Suffice it to say that business executives—male or female—should include in their activities an element of self-promotion to make sure that supervisors and those who govern an organization recognize personal contributions and achievements. (Of course, there are both offensive and appropriate ways to self-promote in the workplace. In Part I, Chapter 10, we discuss communication styles.)

Steps to Consider

Make a list of three milestones you have achieved in the workplace in the last six months. Articulate in a memo to yourself the following elements:

✦ a description of the milestone,

✦ a description of the leadership role you played in achieving this milestone, and

✦ a description of how this milestone positively affects the success of your business.

Then, go have lunch with your Chairperson!

PART I ♦ CHAPTER 2

Cultivating Business Relationships

Invest time in cultivating business relationships—take some action at least once a week. Do not merely be a "doer."

You are a senior executive in a hospital or health care integrated delivery system. You know how important it is to invest time in cultivating business relationships. However, is your reach for business relationships broad enough? How frequently do you do this outreach?

Often, when we move up the corporate ladder within an organization, we do invest time in developing strong business relationships within the organization. However, as we gain more responsibilities within our organizations, we often spend less and less time with our comrades within the organization.

One of the most common ways to formally maintain internal business relationships is through a mentor program. Although research has shown that women can easily identify available mentors, research also shows that a large percentage of women cite lack of mentoring as a major barrier to promotion and career advancement.[2] Similarly, the absence of female role models is cited as one of the major concerns facing the next generation of talent, as this absence has a negative effect on the ambitions of these up and coming leaders.[3] Consequently, it is particularly important for women leaders to make time for

---

[2] Devillard, Sandrine, McKinsey & Company, *Women Matter*, 8 (2007), available at http://www.mckinsey.com/careers/women/makingadifference/socialsectorimpact/womenmatter/.

[3] Devillard, Sandrine, McKinsey & Company, *Women Matter*, 9 (2007), available at http://www.mckinsey.com/careers/women/makingadifference/socialsectorimpact/womenmatter/.

cultivating internal business relationships with other women within the company.

Also, as our management duties require us to interface with outside companies or organizations either doing business or potentially doing business with our firm, we further limit our "discretionary" time spent cultivating strong business relationships both inside and outside of our organizations in order to get the work done.

The more senior we get in management, the more our duties involve outreach to the business community. It could be outreach to current or prospective customers. It could be outreach to our vendors. It could be outreach toward greater company visibility generally. Regardless of the targeted audience, all levels of senior management should view themselves as company ambassadors. Outreach helps your company prosper and, as will be discussed in Part I, Chapter 3, helps with career advancement.

Senior executives should be strategic when cultivating these external business relationships. Sharing meals is the most common venue for cultivating external relationships, but you may want to consider other opportunities that are more convenient for your targeted person. It helps to ask that person when and where he or she prefers to meet.

You also may want to ask yourself whether your targeted audience really is broad enough. We often have a tendency to reach out to people we know well.

Senior executives should make cultivating strong internal and external business relationships a focus and priority for each work week. Within that objective, one should consider both internal business relationships and external business relationships, as the following examples demonstrate.

Example: Cultivate Internal Business Relationships Weekly. Some years ago, our National Health Law Practice established a mentor program for our health law associates. We assign a partner to mentor each associate. The mentor is available to that associate for both professional and personal issues that may arise. The mentor also serves as a resource to that associate for overall career advancement.

I established this mentor program, and during its early years I served as the overall mentor to all of the partner mentors. I also would tell each partner and associate that they always can meet with me on any matter. Most importantly, I would try not to schedule client-related work on Friday afternoons so that I could use that time on my calendar (either scheduled or unscheduled) to address issues that might come up under this program. That way, I could address the issues promptly. I also made it known that there was time built into my calendar for this program. Having a program that encourages people to be proactive about issues and then not carving out time on your calendar to address these issues can send a bad signal about commitment and otherwise seriously undermine the mentoring program's effectiveness.

Example: Cultivate External Business Relationships Weekly. How often have you attended a business event, collected a business card, and never followed up with that person? You do not need to have meals with people to connect with them. Sometimes, just a phone call or email is sufficient to strengthen that initial connection. I keep a separate file with me of those contacts, and review that file weekly to assure follow up with these external contacts. I also give priority to attending events outside my traditional sphere of contacts. For example, once, the parent of one of my son's friends invited me to the annual meeting of the Montgomery County Maryland Chamber of Commerce. I live in Montgomery County, but I had never attended this event before. The incoming president was the head of a large health care delivery system. As a result, the audience included representatives from many health care firms. Just from that event, I have since met individually with several attendees I might never have met otherwise.

Steps to Consider

◆ Review your calendar to see if you have been carving out enough time for cultivating both internal and external business relationships.

◆ If not, designate time for this purpose.

◆ Challenge yourself by seeking very broad ranges of external business contacts beyond the more immediate, and perhaps more comfortable, contacts.

PART I ◆ CHAPTER 3

Being Proactive about Advancement

Be proactive about your advancement.
Take deliberate steps toward your goals.

Have you ever heard of the "glass ceiling?" This phrase was coined many years ago to refer to the limitations set on women's vertical advancement in the workplace. Women were beginning to make inroads into the more junior positions in corporate America. However, there appeared to be both formal policies and informal practices that created barriers to the vertical career advancement of these women. There still are barriers for women and other minorities seeking vertical advancement in the workplace. That is why it is so important to be proactive about your vertical advancement.

A more difficult challenge for women and other minorities is garnering an invitation to the highest echelon of corporate America: the boardroom. The statistics bear this out—women currently hold only 14.7% of board seats of Fortune 500 companies.[4] You already may be a senior executive, at the uppermost echelons of your company, but you may not have been invited into the boardroom that relies on such senior executives. These governance activities help hone a senior executive's skills and expand her business contacts.[5] At the WBL Foundation, we call barriers to this new challenge the "Glass Boardroom Door™." A senior executive's participation in corporate governance at a company other than her or his current employer represents "Horizontal Advancement™."

From my activities with the WBL Foundation, I have learned that recruiting a new board member is quite different from an

---

[4]   *2006 Catalyst Census of Women Board Directors* (www.catalyst.org).
[5]   Refer to Part II for more about this "behind the scenes" review of your resume.

executive search. It often involves a "behind the scenes" review of a candidate under consideration even before that candidate knows that she or he is a potential candidate.

Of course, if you consider Horizontal Advancement™ activities, then you need to "invest time in cultivating business relationships" (discussed in Part I, Chapter 2). These business relationships need to be expansive. It is not enough to reach out and spend time with people in your own company or organization. Take deliberate steps to meet the people who can make advancement and success happen for you.

Steps to Consider

◆ Choose or ask for a mentor or sponsor.

◆ Seek out a confidante or coach.

◆ Think ahead: Where do you want to be 1, 5, and 10 years from now?

◆ Make a list of both your short term and long term advancement goals.

◆ Based upon those goals, what external business relationships do you want to cultivate today in order to achieve both short term and long term goals?

◆ What companies, organizations, or key people are likely to be important for you to reach these goals?

◆ Remember, advancement may be vertical (e.g., promotions) or horizontal (e.g., board positions).

◆ Consider contacting your local Chamber of Commerce and obtain a list of companies operating in your own backyard.

◆ Either from personal or business relationships, identify who you know or could know who could help achieve these goals.

◆ Then, reach out to them and let them know who you are!

PART I ◆ CHAPTER 4

Making your Objectives Known

Make your business and professional objectives known to others, directly or indirectly.

Sometimes what you think is obvious is not obvious to others. It is so difficult to know whether your audience is operating from the same perspective you are. This is especially true for senior executive women. Consider the following scenario:

> *Jane Smith is a CEO of a large non-profit health care system. Jane operates her hospital very successfully. She also provides her board members with very efficient board meetings. On her board are several CEOs of large for profit corporations operating in her service area. Jane has been CEO for over five years, and she is thinking about her Horizontal Advancement™. She is considering seeking a board seat on a for profit board.*

Shouldn't these senior executives automatically consider Jane Smith for a board seat? Isn't being a successful CEO enough or does Jane have to make her interest in corporate governance opportunities known to these CEOs?

Jane should make her corporate governance interests known because it is not always obvious to board members that Horizontal Advancement™ would be of interest to the CEO. This is especially true for women in business leadership positions in companies where past candidates for board seats have normally been non-minority male candidates. The visual frame of reference is historically Caucasian male, so while a male hospital CEO may be considered for such professional opportunities without necessarily having to ask, a female hospital CEO may need to make her interest known to this influential audience.

Sometimes senior executive men perceive a busy senior executive woman as someone not likely to be ambitious or not likely to want this additional professional commitment. Yet these same busy senior executive women may be ready, willing, and interested in this new professional or business challenge.

There are both direct and indirect ways to make your objectives known. In our hypothetical, Jane Smith could speak directly to one of her board members about whether she or he thought it a good idea generally, without specifically asking for a specific seat on a specific board. Or, she could make her interests known to a third party who could deliver the message.

Through my volunteer work for the WBL Foundation, I have learned that board placement is a delicate matter. The nominating committees like to circle around a potential candidate well before any direct approach is made, due to the close relationship board members will have with one another and with senior management. That is why personal recommendations by third parties are key to a board search.

Steps to Consider

- ◆ If you have a business or professional objective you wish to achieve, identify who might help you achieve it.

- ◆ Make your objectives known to others, either directly or indirectly.

- ◆ Be active, not passive, in pursuing your objectives!

PART I ✦ CHAPTER 5

Delegating

Be comfortable with delegating and surround yourself with excellent talent.

Why is it so difficult for some people to delegate work to others in the workplace? Why must some people insist on doing it all by themselves or overlapping with the people who are doing the work anyway? Why do others appear to be so good at delegating the workload? And, why is delegating the workload so important to the long term success of any business organization?

In part, the answers to these questions depend on employee recruitment. Some managers recruit candidates with capabilities less than their own. This may be because the managers, themselves, are not comfortable supervising employees with superior skill sets. Others recruit the best and the brightest because they enjoy the chance to see others step up to the plate and take on more responsibility, and because they know that this helps the organization prosper. Some recruitment styles are obvious and deliberate. Others may be more subtle, or even subconscious. In any event, who and how one recruits new employees affects whether effective delegation takes place.

Consider the following scenario:

Jane Smith is a CEO of a large not-for-profit health care system comprised of five hospitals. On the organizational chart, all five CEOs report directly to her. As each hospital has the same amount of beds, about 125, she initially assumed that each CEO would require about the same amount of supervision and that she would be delegating the same amount of work to each. She has discovered that this is not the case. Jane Smith is finding that she is very much involved in the details of running two of the hospitals. The remaining three hospitals appear to require very little of her time and supervision. The way in which she is spending her time supervising the CEOs of these five hospitals is ad hoc, not based on any advance planning or decision on her part.

Jane well knows that there are only 24 hours in one day and only seven days in a week. Her delegation appears to be uneven. She may know too much about some hospitals and not enough about the others. As the senior executive leader of this system, Jane may want to consider the following questions:

◆ Is the imbalance a function of legitimate workload or is she just more reluctant to delegate responsibility to these two CEOs where she is spending more of her time?

◆ If so, what is it about these two CEOs that makes her more reluctant to delegate responsibilities to them?

◆ Is it that these two CEOs are unwilling to accept the same responsibility as the other CEOs?

◆ With respect to the other three hospitals, is Jane more willing to delegate decisionmaking, or is their independence merely a function of the time limitation and each CEO's particular leadership style?

◆ Should there be some generic list of decisions that are delegated/not delegated so the system operates uniformly?

◆ Is uniformity necessary to achieve success, when there may not be uniformity in the CEOs' respective skill sets?

◆ Should the skill set of the particular employee play a role—either formally or informally—in what decisions and responsibilities are delegated?

These are just some of the key questions raised by this scenario. Depending upon the answers, Jane Smith is in a position to improve the way she delegates the work and how the work actually gets done. Specifically, Jane should consider being in control of the delegation, rather than having the situation control her. Effective delegation is key to the success of any organization.

The issue of delegation often is driven by the level of patience a person has and the amount of enjoyment a person gets in teaching another how to do something, then stepping back to let that student fly solo. Even the worst delegator may be ready, willing, and able to delegate if he or she has confidence (or at least perceives) that the person to whom the work is delegated has excellent skills.

If you want your organization to prosper, you need to satisfy your best employees. As a senior executive, to satisfy these employees, you need to demonstrate to them, through delegation, that you trust them with ever-increasing responsibilities. After all, they are likely to be the next generation you and the governing board rely upon for the future prosperity of your organization.

Steps to Consider

◆ Review your current workload and delegation patterns.

◆ Consider whether you are making the most out of delegating.

◆ Confirm that you have excellent talent for these delegated tasks.

PART I ✦ CHAPTER 6

Striking a Work/Life Balance

Find your work/life balance and help others do the same.
Work/life balance is good for business.

I grew up in Morristown, New Jersey behind the counter of my family's pharmacy. It was literally and figuratively a Mom and Pop pharmacy. We had a pharmacy department, a candy counter, some greeting card displays, a cosmetics counter, and even a liquor department dating back some time. I was one of five daughters with a pharmacist father working long hours and a mother that loved to see her husband and loved to work at the cosmetic/jewelry counter. As a result, we spent a lot of time behind the counters playing and "cleaning" while both of my parents worked at making a living.

I did not realize it at the time, but my family experience as a child was different from most. Many families have a clear line of demarcation between work and family. Often, the husband/father leaves for work and the wife/mother stays home to care for the family. Depending upon the commute, the husband/father may or may not have joined the family for dinner. In my family, there were no such clear lines. Our entire family life revolved around the family business.

When I joined Epstein Becker & Green in September 1979 as a single woman, I did not at first understand the importance of making a line of demarcation between work and home. I just worked. In those days, without computers and the Internet, if I was going to work, I needed to be physically in the office—which is what I did. Day after day. Weekends too. After the first few years, I came to realize that, even as a single person, I needed a balance between work and non-work. Although I loved the work I was doing, and I enjoyed the people in the firm, I also needed another focus. Over time, I became involved in a Jewish charity organization. I volunteered my time and eventually met my husband in that context.

Then the years become a blur. I got married and had two children right away. My husband was a private lawyer at the same time, and we both continued to work full time as lawyers and raise two children with a housekeeper at home. Nine years later, we added a third child to the mix. By then, our parents were starting to need our time and our two older children were in middle school, needing more of our attention. It was then that my husband and I decided that he would become a stay-at-home dad. His focus on the home at that time helped me keep my focus on work and yet have a good work/life balance. (Indeed, in our Women Business Leaders Foundation, I have met many senior executive women who have spouses who stay home to take care of family—both children and parents!)

Affirmatively planning and seeking such a work/life balance is even more essential today than in previous years—especially in two career families. With the advent of new technologies, office work has invaded our homes. Indeed, if you want to instant message a senior executive of a company, the best time to do so is between 9:00 PM and 11:00 PM Sunday evenings—many of us read our emails at that time to get ready for the next work week that is about to begin.

Yet, I know that many leaders in companies are reluctant to show their "life-balance" side in the workplace. To a large degree, this is in response to a corporate model that "equates leadership with unfailing availability and total geographic mobility," which is seen as incompatible with the work and domestic responsibilities facing women.[6] Some believe that management should be hard-charging and work-focused to set a

---

[6]   Devillard, Sandrine, McKinsey & Company, *Women Matter*, 7 (2007), available at http://www.mckinsey.com/careers/women/ makingadifference/socialsectorimpact/womenmatter/.

tone for others in the work setting. Others believe that it is not necessary to bring personal matters into the workplace.

In my view, it is important for a leader to show that she or he does have a life outside the workplace and that she or he expects others to do the same. Otherwise, more junior employees may not like what they see in terms of what the future holds for them in the organization. The question is when and how to demonstrate a work/life balance.

One of the best practices I have used has been to keep a "life" calendar at work. My "life" calendar reflects both family and work obligations. It includes key dates for parent/teacher conferences, key sporting events for my children, key dates for plays, etc. If there is something confidential happening at home, this is marked "private" but it is on my "life" calendar, on view for others at work to see. This way, if at all possible, I can avoid having a work obligation scheduled during a time that conflicts with a family matter.

Second, I often share the accomplishments of my children with my work team. When my son, Isaac, played ice hockey in high school during his junior year, his high school team won the state championship. Everyone on my work team knew when I was leaving early to attend some of the playoff games, and they were rooting for his team with me.

Third, I ask my work team about their non-work lives. I enjoy hearing about their children's achievements and personal hobbies. You spend so much time with work colleagues that, in my view, it is more natural to ask about the life side of their day than not to ask about it.

Finally, I have made it known that there is a "sacred time" during the week that is off limits to intrusions—if at all possible. In my life, this is Friday evening. My family celebrates the Sabbath on Friday evening by having dinner in the dining room (with a tablecloth and cloth napkins!). We often have family or friends to visit. I do no work that evening. This sacred time requires a certain amount of discipline on the part of all members of the family, and that discipline has paid off. We have enjoyed many years of rewarding Friday night dinners. These dinners mark for me a transition from work to non-work, both physically and mentally.

Steps to Consider

◆ A well rested and balanced person is good for business. Find your balance and, as a business leader in your organization, make sure to help others do the same.

◆ Review your calendar to see if you would be better off integrating your "home" calendar with your work calendar to create a "life" calendar in order to better monitor your work/life balance.

◆ Discuss work/life balance issues with your colleagues at work.

◆ Review your traditional week and see if you have enough time carved out for rest, rejuvenation, and personal relationships.

◆ If not, you may want to carve out your own sacred time to make sure you have enough time for the life-side of your balance.

PART I ◆ CHAPTER 7

Informal Networking

Create your own meeting. Informal networking can be just as effective as formal networking. You do not need to wait for meetings or retreats to network with others relevant to your business.

Everyone seems to know instinctively that you will do better in business if you know more people, and if more people know you. Yet, we all seem to get into the slump of getting the work done and thus limiting the time for meeting new people. If you only focus on just doing the work, the only people who will know you are the people with you when you are getting your work done.

If you are a senior executive from a hospital, you most likely eat lunch with other senior executives from the same hospital. What would happen if you were to have lunch with someone from a different hospital in the same system? You would find out more about what may be happening in the system. You might learn about issues your system colleague is facing—ones that you are not yet confronting at your facility or that you could avoid. In turn, your system colleague will hear about your issues and learn more about who you are and how you are handling matters.

Networking is a best practice in business precisely because it facilitates access to information and people in the business marketplace. And let's face it, information and people are key to many successes.

The problem is that many people falsely believe that they need structure in order to network effectively. They are likely to reach out to others only in a format created for outreach. Those formats often come in the form of conferences or established periodic meetings—like quarterly updates or even board meetings. These are known events, with dates, times, and places. While they definitely provide opportunities for business people to network, these meetings are usually few and far between. They also come with a set attendee list, when you may want to create your own invitation list for business purposes.

That explains why number seven of WBL's Ten Best Practices for Advancing Women in Business is informal networking. Informal networking can be just as effective as formal networking. Indeed, it can be more effective. You do not need to wait for meetings or retreats to network with others relevant to your business. You can establish the time, place, topic, and invitation list. Just create your own meeting!

Steps to Consider

◆ Set aside at least one meal per week to network with someone outside of your normal work circles.

◆ Create a meeting at a restaurant and ask disparate people to attend—let everyone know that they only pay for themselves. At WBL, we call these BYOCC™ dinners—Bring Your Own Credit Card dinners. That way, the cost of the meal is not borne on any one person's budget, and finances are not the barrier to getting together.

◆ Make the most of a business conference. You may want to email potential attendees before you arrive to make plans for meeting key people for private meetings, rather than take the chance that they either won't attend or get tied up with other appointments.

✦ Make internet introductions. You can do this at your desk. You introduce one person you know to another person you know. You set forth their respective contact information and, if they need help starting a conversation, you explain to them why you thought they should know each other. You will find that because you are frequently visible with your contacts, others will introduce you, or at least think of you, when business opportunities arise.

✦ No matter what, stay in touch with people. Consider their needs and be helpful. You never know when someone will return the favor.

PART I ◆ CHAPTER 8

Passing Opportunities Along

*When you are not interested in an opportunity,
make recommendations and pass the information along.
Every opportunity that comes your way is an
opportunity for someone.*

One of the main purposes of my Women Business Leaders Foundation is to give senior executive women from the U.S. health care industry the opportunity to be selected for board seats on for profit company boards. After all, becoming a director represents the chance to participate at the highest echelon of where business gets done. To that end, we have reached out to various search firms that specialize in these unique searches. The search firm personnel alert us when they have a potential search. We announce it via email to more than 1,700 WBL senior executive women. The women self-select; only those interested reply with their resumes. We do not screen these resumes. We just collect them and send them off to the search firm. We find out later whether one of our candidates was chosen.

When we went through this process recently, to our surprise, we got a resume from a man who requested that his resume be included for consideration along with the resumes from other women. It made us pause for a moment. On the one hand, we are trying to increase gender diversity of boards by providing women candidates because boards are currently male domi-nated. Forwarding a man's resume seemed, at first, inconsistent with our goals. However, upon further thought, we were excited about including a man's resume because it meant that one of the WBL women who had received the call for candidates had followed one of our Ten Best Practices. When you are not interested in an opportunity, make recommendations and pass the information along. Every opportunity that comes your way is an opportunity for someone.

This man was able to reply to our call for board candidates only because a WBL Foundation Associate had forwarded the email to him. In this particular circumstance, the expertise that the company sought was somewhat narrow, and the man had the type of experience that was the subject of the search. The woman who passed along the opportunity is now perceived as a "player" in the eyes of that man. She was able to expand his opportunities; that would not have been the case if she had simply deleted the email from her inbox. Even if the man does not get the director position, he likely will consider the WBL Foundation Associate's referral to be of value because it gave him visibility with the search firm for other future searches. It is not every day that you find out about a potential board position for your particular expertise. Of course, we went ahead and put the man's resume in with the others, consistent with our "no-prescreening" process.

In business, opportunities are presented from time to time. Whether the opportunity is a job search, a board search, or information about a company up for sale, it is usually the case that these opportunities are not attractive to you. However, whether you are interested is only the beginning of the inquiry. Do not let the inquiry stop with you. The next inquiry should be whether you know someone else who could be interested.

Opportunities are a form of "business currency." Do not forget to get credit for passing the opportunity along. If you pass the opportunity along without getting credit, you lose some of the value. That means that *you* should be the one who forwards the email to the potential candidate and copies the person offering the opportunity. Make it clear that you are the one making the introduction. If you simply ask the person offering the opportunity to "just mention my name," you take the chance that your referral may not be credited to you.

The objective of this best practice is to pay attention to opportunities in a more formal way, and to make sure that you get the most from them—even if you, yourself, have no interest. Hopefully, if you use this business currency to help someone else, someday someone else will use this business currency to help you.

Steps to Consider

- ✦ Identify a recent opportunity that you let "die" at your desk.

- ✦ See if there is still time to resurrect it by passing it along.

- ✦ If so, go ahead and pass it on to someone.

- ✦ Be sure to respond to everyone who calls you with an opportunity, regardless of how irrelevant it may appear to be.

- ✦ See if there is any way you can help, even if you are not the right person for that opportunity.

PART I ◆ CHAPTER 9

Learning from Challenges

*Learn from challenges. Failures are just challenges.
You can learn a lot from challenges.*

I am sure that you have heard this cliché before—that failures are just challenges and that you can learn a lot from challenges. Yet, in my view, there really are no failures in the business world—at least not in the same way one can fail a test in school. Instead, there are only challenges. There are so many variables that play a role in the outcome of any business event; one person cannot really and truly control a significant business outcome, and therefore cannot count the outcome as a failure. Even the most hands-on CEO must admit that she does not control everything that makes the company a success—or she is just fooling herself.

I think that the WBL Foundation Associates identified "Learning from Challenges" as a best practice because successful people in business address challenges all the time, but they take the time to learn from their most challenging events at work. They also do not shy away from making the necessary decisions at some of the most stressful moments of business decisionmaking. Whatever the health care industry management challenge—acquisition of a hospital or physician practice group, a governmental investigation, a major termination of a key employee, etc.—successful leaders identify that they are facing a major challenge, and recognize the additional steps that may prove helpful under such trying circumstances.

In my professional work, I deal with such challenges more frequently than others because of the nature of my law practice.

My expertise is in Medicare and Medicaid issues, which includes defending companies and organizations being investigated for health care fraud. There are days when I get a call that FBI agents are making a surprise visit to a client with a search warrant. Other days, I may get a call from a lawyer from the U.S. Department of Justice who asks me to have one of our clients come in "to chat" about a new matter. In any event, I am there not only to defend the client but also to help the client navigate through the maze of enforcement and compliance. The ultimate outcome can run the gamut from having the government just "go away" all the way to a criminal conviction and exclusion from future participation in government programs.

I mention this type of work because, in these very stressful and trying circumstances, my job is to try to achieve the best outcome under the circumstances. Yet, my ability to achieve that outcome is dependent on so many important variables. For example, in addition to the underlying facts—an obvious and very important variable—there are the less obvious but still very important variables such as the cooperation and focus of the client, the acumen of the client's decisionmakers, the talent of the lawyers and staff working for the government, the credibility of any whistleblower, and even the effectiveness of that whistleblower's counsel. Indeed, there are times when one of these variables plays an even greater role than the facts and law of the case.

When one of the cases ends (which is usually, but not always, with a settlement), I call it a "closing." I use that term the same way one would close on buying a piece of real estate or close on an acquisition or investment in a company. There are final documents to sign, money to wire, maybe even press releases to issue. No matter what business you are in, one of the most important steps at a closing is to take a break and reflect on the matter with those people that were involved on your side of the matter—how it began, how it was handled, what the outcome was, and what you can learn from the matter. This is so important for getting better at what you do—a continuous challenge for anyone in business, regardless of seniority.

Steps to Consider

◆ Recognize when you are facing a serious challenge and consider all of the major variables that can influence the outcome of that challenge.

◆ Once you have identified the major variables, you are in a better position to consider what steps could affect the outcome positively and whether you have control over those steps.

◆ Remember to take a moment for a closing once a major challenge has passed—or create such a moment if one is not that defined—so that the work team can reflect on what has occurred. This learning process is relevant regardless of seniority. It prepares everyone to take on the next challenge more successfully.

PART I ✦ CHAPTER 10

Focusing on Communication Styles

Focus on communication styles. Become knowledgeable about differences in communication styles. Know your audience and communicate in their style.

Communication skills comprise a skill set that we all use every day in the business world. Yet, it surprises me to find out how many people have not studied the science and art of communication. I never took a course on communication during my formal education. Instead, I chose to read some books on the subject. It was an eye-opener for me; there is so much valuable and insightful information on this subject not put to use in the business world.

As a managing attorney in a major law firm, you can imagine how important it is for me to communicate well with the hundreds of people I manage directly or indirectly. Yes, it helps that we are all lawyers with a similar education and frame of reference, but there still are differences that require adjustments to guarantee that any message is sent or received well. For example, some attorneys are more computer literate and do well with short messages, while others are more detail-oriented and prefer a written memo that they can digest in more detail.

I also have many clients in the health care and life sciences industry. Many of the clients have in-house attorneys. The communication to these attorneys is similar, but not always the same as within the firm. It depends upon the in-house attorney's level of knowledge of the regulatory area likely to be the subject of our conversation. Some in-house lawyers are generalists, while some are specialists. You want to present your information according to the recipient's level of expertise.

We also have many health care clients who do not have in-house lawyers. This means that, at any time, the person triaging a project to us may be someone without legal training. I need to be effective in getting the right information from that person and sending the right information back to that person in this context as well.

Another consideration is that not all clients are computer savvy or computer focused. Some clients only want us to communicate via email while others prefer voice mail. Some clients want short summaries, while others want major white papers. In these types of service relationships, effective managers address the communicating mechanisms, as well as the content.

As a Medicare/Medicaid attorney, I also need to communicate effectively with the law enforcement community—U.S. Department of Justice attorneys, FBI agents, Office of Inspector General personnel, and state enforcement personnel. These communications require not only a high level of accuracy, but also an advocacy element.

We studied effective communication at our first WBL Summit. In small groups, Summit attendees viewed the video "Talking 9 to 5: Women and Men in the Workplace," by Deborah Tannen, Ph.D. Tannen is a linguistics Professor in the College of Arts & Sciences at Georgetown University in Washington, D.C.. She has extensively published, both in the academic and popular arenas, and her books on this subject are excellent and highly recommended. After viewing the videotape, attendees discussed the presentation and recommended best practices.

Some comments were priceless. For example, one attendee commented that, while we try so hard in the workplace to treat men and women on equal terms, we neglect the fact that most men and women bring to the table very different communication styles which can impede work and corporate advancement.

Awareness of these differences goes a long way toward becoming more productive.

Another commenter found it so true that men are more likely to speak directly about what they want, while women are more likely to speak indirectly. The indirectness causes misunderstandings.

Finally, I remember how one woman commented that if she had seen the tape years before, she might still have been married to her former husband! Little did she know that he actually may have been listening to her while reading the newspaper, since men are less likely to require eye contact in a listening mode while women are more likely to require visual connection.

In my law practice, I often tell my colleagues that fifty percent of the project is getting to the right legal answer or right legal judgment. The other fifty percent is how we communicate that outcome to the client or to third parties on behalf of the client. I think that this tenet applies in other occupational settings as well. Indeed, if you study communication styles and follow some of the basic principles behind the "science" of communication, you will be much more effective in all parts of your life.

Steps to Consider

- ✦ Become aware of different communication styles.

- ✦ Consider how these different communication styles affect the workplace.

- ✦ For a more productive and efficient workplace, make sure the employees of your business also become aware of different communication styles.

- ✦ Take into account the communication style of your targeted audience when you are attempting to negotiate a particular outcome.

PART II

Breaking the Glass Boardroom Door™

THE GLASS BOARDROOM DOOR™:
Similar to the "glass ceiling" (informal barriers to advancement for women in the workplace), the glass boardroom door is a clear yet difficult barrier for women to cross into the corporate boardroom. In this context, women are not moving up–through a ceiling–and advancing in the hierarchy of their organization. Instead, women are attempting to cross into peer opportunities–such as board service–in other organizations without leaving their day jobs. Board service reflects Horizontal Advancement™ as opposed to vertical advancement.

PART II ◆ INTRODUCTION

*The Ten Best Practices for Making the Board Nominating Committee's Radar Screen**

One of WBL's missions is to help senior executive women grow professionally *even after* they are in senior management. One form of Horizontal Advancement™ is serving as an outside director of a for profit corporation.

Yet, there is a "Glass Boardroom Door™" that needs to be broken. According to Catalyst, a non-profit organization dedicated to advancing women in business, women hold only 14.6% of the board seats at Fortune 500 companies. This is amazing when you consider that half of all of America's consumers are women. Even more amazing is that in the health care industry, where women make three out of every four household healthcare decisions, women hold nowhere near that percentage of the board seats.

Reeling from a string of corporate accounting scandals, America's chief executives and board nominating committees are focused on recruiting directors that are more independent: people who are tough, knowledgeable, and at all costs honest. However, two important questions remain largely unanswered:

1. Will there be enough capable executives willing to accept the dramatically increased scrutiny and potential liability certain to go with serving on a corporate board?

2. Will the drive toward board reform finally result in the greater diversity—specifically gender diversity—that has been severely deficient over the years?

---

* Portions of this introduction were initially published on September 30, 2002 as an opinion article by Lynn Shapiro Snyder in *Modern Healthcare*, entitled "The Glass Boardroom Ceiling: Women have the know-how to solve corporate crises but aren't getting the chance."

I hope the answer to both questions is "yes."

As an outside legal counsel who often works closely with senior executives and board members, I know that there are plenty of talented and capable people, both male and female. But are they willing to serve as outside directors? Will boards be willing to consider candidates from senior management other than sitting or retired CEOs for board service? If the answer to both of these questions is "yes," then this convergence should result in boards that are more diverse.

But, does board gender diversity really matter?

Yes.

Research demonstrates that gender diversity in the boardroom leads to favorable results in the boardroom—better decisionmaking and a more profitable corporation.

According to a report by the Conference Board of Canada,[1] which examined the "impact of women's contributions in six key areas of good governance practice," proved that "board processes differ when diverse perspectives are brought to the boardroom table," leading to vastly different outcomes.[2]

Consider the following data from the Conference Board of Canada's Report[3]:

Organizations with Boards Including Two or More Women	Organizations with All Male Boards
Board adopts on average 2.64 of 5 accountability best practices	Board adopts on average 1.51 of 5 accountability best practices
Board reviews 5 or more nonfinancial performance measures regularly	Board reviews 2.5 nonfinancial performance measures regularly

continues

---

[1] Vanessa Anastapoulous, David Brown & Debra Brown, Conference Board of Canada, *Women on Boards: Not Just the Right Thing…The Bright Thing* (2002).

[2] *Id.*

[3] *Id.* at ii.

Organizations with Boards Including Two or More Women	Organizations with All Male Boards
Board explicitly assumes 94% of responsibilities recommended by TSE*	Board explicitly assumes 72% of responsibilities recommended by TSE
Gender representation is number two selection criterion for board	Gender representation is number nine selection criterion for board

*Toronto Stock Exchange

Studies conducted in the United States by Oklahoma State University[4] and the Wellesley Centers for Women[5] have concluded that corporate boards with several women engage in better decisionmaking and take more perspectives and conditions into account in meetings. In 2006, the Wellesley Centers for Women introduced the concept of "critical mass" on boards which asserts that having three or more women on corporate boards enhances all aspects of board operation. Women directors bring a different type of leadership to the table. This different type of leadership creates a better boardroom dynamic, resulting in more positive problem solving, better decisionmaking, and improved collaboration among board members.

A 2007 Catalyst study later confirmed the quantitative effects of these new boardroom dynamics. The study found that "companies with more women board directors experience higher financial performance" when compared with companies that have few, if any, women on their boards. Specifically, Catalyst found that those companies with three or more women board directors experienced "notably stronger than average" performance, boasting a Return on Equity, a Return on Sales, and a Return on Invested Capital that outperformed the average by 53, 42, and 66 percent, respectively.[6]

[4] David Carter, Betty Simkins & W. Gary Simpson, Corporate Governance, Board Diversity, and Firm Value, *The Financial Review*, Vol. 38 (2003).
[5] Wellesley Centers for Women, *Critical Mass on Corporate Boards: Why Three or More Women Enhance Governance*, 37 (2006).
[6] Catalyst, 2007 The Bottom Line: Connecting Corporate Performance and Women's Representation on Boards, (2007) http://www.catalyst.org (last visited October 2, 2007).

Given recently enacted corporate reforms, it makes business sense to address the lack of gender diversity in corporate boardrooms. Having diverse points of view on a board yields a wider and better approach to decisionmaking. Further, more effective boards promote more compliant and more profitable companies.

Unfortunately, generally speaking, corporate boardrooms have not yet embraced gender diversity. One reason often proffered is the allegedly insufficient supply of senior executive women with experience comparable to male board members. Others argue that if such women exist, they are overcommitted to multiple boards, unwilling to serve because of time commitments, or risk-averse. These statements are not supported by the facts.

In the past few years, a critical mass of senior executive women finally has reached top positions throughout various industries. As the women cap their careers, they are ready to share the risks and rewards of governing boards of directors with their male counterparts, giving back to other companies by sharing their knowledge and experience.

However, in seeking such board positions, women have discovered that chief executive officers and nominating committees often recruit based upon a "whom do you know" and "who knows you" culture. For the vast majority of these women, business contacts—while they may be deep within their own companies or industries—fail to garner the visibility necessary to cross the radar screens of CEOs and nominating committees.

Indeed, in a recent survey conducted by the WBL Foundation, 54.5% of WBL Foundation Associates surveyed found exclusion from formal networks to be the greatest barrier to having more women serving on corporate for profit boards. Another 22.7% found "lack of mentoring" to be another one of the significant challenges facing women interested in serving on corporate boards.[7]

Part II will highlight ten best practices that potential women corporate directors may want to follow in order to increase their visibility, readiness, and capabilities to serve on for profit company boards.

---

[7]   Women Business Leaders of the U.S. Health Care Industry Foundation,™ *2008 WBL Report* (2008).

**Ten Best Practices for Making the Board
Nominating Committee's Radar Screen**

1. Get line experience.

2. Fill in gaps in your knowledge.

3. Package yourself.

4. Consider smaller local companies or non-profit boards as stepping stones.

5. Be realistic about the time you have to commit.

6. State your governance goal to others and ask for advice.

7. Network with current board members.

8. Consult the experts: board search consultants.

9. Start the conversation about gender diversity in the boardroom.

10. Be an advocate for diversity in the boardroom.

As in Part I of this book, although many examples that follow may be from the health care industry, these principles are applicable to other industry sectors. I hope this information helps you achieve your Horizontal Advancement™ goals related to board governance.[8]

---

[8] Another book for potential new board members is *Answering the Call: Understanding the Duties, Risks and Rewards of Corporate Governance,* co-authored by Lynn Shapiro Snyder and Robert D. Reif. Visit www.womenleadinghealthcare.org to learn how to obtain a copy.

PART II ◆ CHAPTER 1

Get Line Experience.

Most CEOs and nominating committees want board candidates who are sitting CEOs or very recently retired CEOs. This is because such executives are likely to have had the broadest experience in running a company. Directors are supposed to be a resource to management, and so such broad experience is preferred.

Nevertheless, more and more companies are limiting the number of boards that their sitting CEO may serve on at any one time—assuming that the CEO is permitted to serve on any outside boards at all! As a result, boards are beginning to consider senior executives immediately below the CEO position. Despite this initial shift, it remains preferable for the board candidate to have held profit and loss responsibility for a company or for a division of a company.

To satisfy this preference, if you currently are in a staff position, you may wish to consider taking a temporary or more permanent assignment where you can get profit and loss work experience. If that is not possible, determine whether your current staff position requires budgetary accountability and if so, be sure to describe this in your board resume, along with any other significant business related achievements.

In addition to profit and loss experience, some CEOs and nominating committees value certain special expertise, such as experience with information systems, government/public policy, or international business in today's global marketplace. Be sure to highlight in your board resume these valuable areas of expertise in addition to whatever operational experience you bring to the boardroom table. Indeed, you may want to target your board searches to those companies, industries, and industry sectors where your particular area of expertise is likely to be especially attractive.

PART II ✦ CHAPTER 2

Address Your Knowledge Gaps.

Not everyone in senior management majored in business or finance in school. Consequently, there may be gaps in your educational background that serve as challenges to managing businesses effectively—let alone governing at the board level. Even if you did study business or finance, you may not know the most current information.

To address these potential knowledge gaps, consider attending executive educational programs to strengthen your weak spots, especially if your weak spots are financial skills. These programs are also a great place to network.

Many universities hold programs and conferences relating to corporate governance and furthering one's governance-related knowledge. There are excellent programs sponsored by academic institutes, professional associations, and non-profit groups. These programs prepare new corporate directors for the boardroom and educate current board members as well.[9]

Programs sponsored by various professional and non-profit groups include the following:

✦ **National Association of Corporate Directors**
   www.nacdonline.org
   NACD is a non-profit membership organization dedicated to corporate governance. NACD holds educational events at a large number of chapters around the United States. (Membership is open to all board members or potential board members, male or female.)

---

[9]   List of Academic Programs from
      www.change-leaders.com/board_training.html.

✦ **Women Corporate Directors**
www.womencorporatedirectors.com
WCD is a national community of women corporate
directors who meet for regional dinners, at national conferences, and by email for updates—to distribute board
opportunities, and to conduct surveys. WCD now includes
members on 500 boards. Membership in WCD, a for-profit
professional organization, is limited to current or recent
corporate directors.

✦ **Boardroom Bound www.boardroombound.biz**
This non-profit organization focuses on educating a supply
of diversity candidates—including male minority candidates—for board service. It is not necessary to be a corporate
director to participate in Boardroom Bound's programs.

✦ **On-Board Bootcamp**
Contact Susan Stautberg of PartnerCom
Corporation at partcom@verizon.net
This organization provides an insider's guide on how to be
selected as a corporate director and introduces board
candidates to experienced directors and search executives
who share the lessons they have learned along the way.

Programs sponsored by academic institutions include
the following:

✦ **Director's Education Institute at Duke University**
www.fuqua.duke.edu/conference/dei/index.html

✦ **Harvard—The Corporate Governance Series**
www.exed.hbs.edu/programs/cgs.html

✦ **Northwestern University's Kellogg School of Management**
www.kellogg.northwestern.edu/execed/programs/
governance.htm
The Kellogg School includes a Center for Executive
Women and a Director Development Institute specifically
for women.

✦ **Stanford Directors' Forum**
   www.gsb.stanford.edu/exed/sdf/index.html

✦ **University of Pennsylvania Wharton Programs**
   executiveeducation.wharton.upenn.edu/oe/index.cfm

Attending one or more of these executive/board service development programs helps expand your knowledge about good corporate governance practices. You also have the unique opportunity to meet other board member contacts. See Part II, Chapter 7 for more information and suggestions on making the most out of these unique opportunities, both as networking and as educational events.

PART II ◆ CHAPTER 3

Package Yourself for Board Service.

Preparing for board service is different from preparing for employment consideration. You want to create a board resume that emphasizes the experiences and leadership areas you will bring into the boardroom, regardless of your place of employment. According to the various board search experts who have spoken at WBL events, you only have several minutes—if that—to catch the attention of the board recruiter or nominating committee member who glances at your board resume.

As mentioned in Part II, Chapter 1, your board resume should provide a snapshot of your line experience and any special expertise that you would like that board to consider. Your board resume also should mention any corporate governance programs that you have completed, especially if you participated in these programs to address weak spots on your resume.

You also should consider how you appear to your intended audience. In working with various nominating committees and board search firms, I have learned that boards circle a candidate for some time before approaching him or her. They will Google the candidate, and take note of the networking groups, affiliations, and other boards listed on your board resume. Consider what they will find when they circle around you.

Your board resume also should include accomplishments in volunteer and non-profit board work, as well as accomplishments in employment. Self-promotion needs to be accurate and comprehensive. You want to highlight your operational credentials, proven results, crisis management skills, and industry knowledge.

You also want to keep your board resume updated as you continue to add to your experiences—and be sure that others have an updated copy as well.

PART II ✦ CHAPTER 4

Consider Using Local and Non-profit Boards as Stepping Stones.

Some smaller local companies, non-profit boards, and even advisory boards may help you gain entrée into for profit boards of larger companies later. Sometimes the best experience for board service is, not surprisingly, service on another board. Research supports the fact that once a woman joins one board, she often is invited to join others. According to Catalyst in 2006, fewer than 600 women held the 827 Fortune 500 board seats held by women—and these are Fortune 500 board seats alone.[10] Undoubtedly, these women sit on various boards, including non-profit boards and the boards of companies in their community. This is how board membership—sometimes even in a non-profit capacity—can place you on a "pre-approved list."

Service on any board creates an informal networking opportunity for you to get to know other leaders in the community and, more importantly, for them to get to know you. In the course of networking, you can make your further governance objectives known. You should cultivate these relationships often, as mentioned earlier Part I, Chapter 2, and take steps to advance your governance goals the same way you strategically advance your company's goals.

However, if your ultimate goal is to serve on a for profit board, you should choose among non-profit board opportunities carefully. Some non-profit boards are comprised of for profit CEOs who can be a valuable resource. Other non-profit boards may be very time-consuming without providing good business

---

[10]   Calculated from the *2006 Catalyst Census of Women Board Directors of the Fortune 500* (2006), available at www.catalyst.org.

networking opportunities. Local chambers of commerce and other similar business organizations can be a good source of information about the profit and non-profit firms that operate in your locality.

In some instances, the same people who eventually will put together a company's board of directors choose the advisory board. These advisory boards are a good way to make your governance goals known and to expand your networking circle. They also can be a unique way to utilize very specific areas of expertise. However, as with non-profit boards, you should choose carefully and investigate the advantages and disadvantages of joining these boards as you would any other type of board. You should be certain that the time you spend working with these companies is justified by the benefits and networking opportunities such companies can provide.

PART II ✦ CHAPTER 5

Be Realistic About the Time You Have to Commit.

There are only 24 hours in a day. You should assess how much time you have to be a positive, contributing member of a board, especially if your current employment is more than full time.

This is especially true since the Sarbanes-Oxley federal legislation changed the rules for publicly traded companies. Board service requires more time and focus than ever before. If you are one of the financial experts on a board, as required by Sarbanes-Oxley, you are expected to be more alert than ever. If you are on a board outside your own industry, where your expertise is applicable, but where you do not work every day, you should bring yourself up to speed on industry facts and happenings.

Interestingly, some companies may not permit a senior executive to serve on an outside board. The explanation for this prohibition often is cloaked in terms of avoiding conflicts and conflicting time commitments. Yet, conflicts can be addressed on a case by case basis, and the outside board experience often gives the senior executive new insights that have value for his or her employer. It is important, however, to have not only the permission, but also the support of your current employer as you seek Horizontal Advancement™ in the context of board service. You should consider the fact that you will have a minimum of four board meetings per year, in addition to committee obligations, necessary teleconferences, and travel and preparation time.

In any event, remember the need for work/life balance by keeping one "life" calendar (see Part I, Chapter 6 for more). Be honest in your assessment of your available time to provide conscientious board service.

PART II ◆ CHAPTER 6

State Your Governance Goals and Ask for Advice.

It is not obvious to men that a senior executive woman may want the opportunity for board service. There are likely many reasons for this, but the one that comes to my mind is that women are not obvious board candidates because women have historically not been in the boardroom.

As stated in Part I, Chapter 4, it has been my experience that women more likely have to state their corporate governance goals in order to be sure that male colleagues know of their intentions. While it seems obvious to senior executive women that they would be interested in board service, it may not be obvious to the rest of the world. If you tell other executives and board members that you are interested in serving on a board of directors, they may be able to provide you specific advice and/ or introduce you to someone in their network circle that could lead to board service.

Consider again the advice I shared in Part I, Chapter 8, Passing the Opportunity Along. A good way to state your governance goal may be to pass along a board opportunity for which you do not fit on to a colleague who *is* a good fit. In response to one of our recent WBL "board opportunity" emails, we received an email from a woman in senior management, asking if she could share the opportunity with her CEO, who was a man. We encouraged her to share this opportunity with her CEO as a form of "business currency." However, when she did so, he encouraged her to submit her own resume instead. By sharing the opportunity, she not only made her governance goals known, but gained his support. The CEO will now think of her for future board positions he hears about.

Some other ways to make your governance goals known are to:

+ keep your board resume updated, and include a section on your board resume listing the volunteer activities and boards on which you currently serve;

+ attend educational and networking events (such as those mentioned in Part II, Chapter 2) where you will meet other potential director candidates, and, by virtue of attending, make your governance goals known; and

+ maintain your board resume in the databases of various board search firms and candidate supply organizations.

PART II ◆ CHAPTER 7

Broaden Your Networking Circle to Include Current Board Members.

Board members make recommendations and clearly play a leadership role in selecting the next new board member. You should get to know these board members. Set time aside each week or month for networking with one of these people, who are likely outside of your usual networking circle. So how do you go about finding board members to include in your circle?

Sometimes it helps to target certain companies for board service based upon your expertise and geographic location. Make a list of companies in your local industry, including as broad a range of entities as possible. Once you identify these companies, you may be able to find out who the current board members are by reviewing the company's website or press releases. If the company has publicly traded debt or equity, there are government filings that contain board listings. Once you know who the board members are, you are in a position specifically to target your networking circles to include one or more of these particular board members.

In the alternative, you may want to join organizations or attend conferences where board members are likely to be. At these meetings, you will likely meet a broad range of current board members. Hearing current board members speak at conferences also provides you with an opportunity to follow up on such contact with correspondence or through mutual friends.

Increasing numbers of senior executive women are successfully targeting local organizations and attending conferences to network, sharpen skills, share information on best practices, and receive advice on how to land a position on corporate boards.

PART II ◆ CHAPTER 8

Consult the Experts: Board Search Consultants.

With the advent of the Sarbanes-Oxley Act, nominating committees increasingly are turning to professional board search consultants to help them find new board members. Many executive search firms have a special team of search consultants focused on board searches. Indeed, at each of our WBL Summits, we hold a panel discussion featuring several of these consultants, who discuss various trends and issues relating to their ever-growing board search practices.

You may wish to consider scheduling a private meeting with board search consultants in your area. At a minimum, be sure your board resume is in their database and that someone at the firm knows who you are. Not all board searches are done through these board search firms, but more are being done this way, and a board is often more likely to invite a "diverse" candidate by using a board search firm.

You can visit www.womenleadinghealthcare.org to view a list of board search experts known to WBL.

PART II ✦ CHAPTER 9

Start the Conversation about Gender Diversity in the Boardroom.

It has been our experience that many executives, male or female, at various levels, either are not aware of or have not considered the fact that there is only one woman—or zero women—on their board of directors. Only by increasing awareness of the lack of gender diversity in the boardroom will women obtain more than the 14.6% of board seats (of the Fortune 500) that they currently hold. In Europe, this statistic is even worse, with women holding only 11% of corporate board seats throughout Europe.[11]

Starting a conversation about gender diversity in the boardroom—while similar to stating your personal governance goal—can have additional benefits such as increasing the number of board searches where gender diversity is considered and putting women candidates on the board's radar screen. Talking points for this conversation appear on the next page.

---

[11]   Devillard, Sandrine, McKinsey & Company, *Women Matter*, 6 (2007), available at http://www.mckinsey.com/careers/women/ makingadifference/socialsectorimpact/womenmatter/.

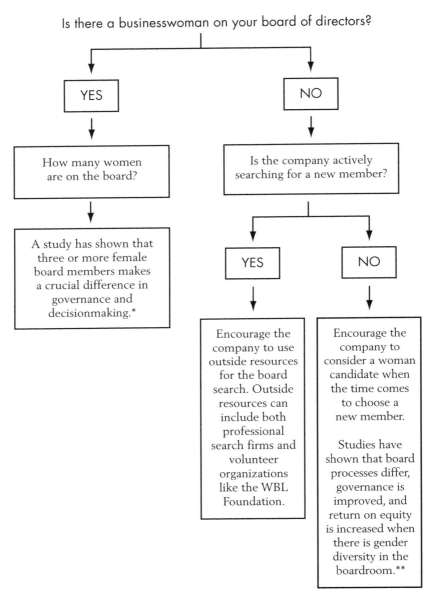

* This 2006 study, *Critical Mass on Corporate Boards: Why Three or More Women Enhance Governance*, published by the Wellesley Centers for Women, is available online at www.wcwonline.org.

** A 2007 Catalyst study, *The Bottom Line, Corporate Performance and Women on Boards*, is available on Catalyst's website at www.catalyst.org.

PART II ◆ CHAPTER 10

Be an Advocate for Diversity in the Boardroom.

Everyone has some type of relationship with a for profit corporation. You may be an owner or an investor. You may be an employee. At a minimum, you are a consumer of a company's products and services. (After all, women have been found to be the "driving force behind more than 70% of household decisions").[12]

Do you know who sits on the board of these various companies? Do you know whether there is gender diversity in the boardroom? At today's rate of growth, it will be 2079 before women hold 50% of corporate board seats.[13] It is necessary for each of us, in our own way, to become advocates for gender diversity and take the opportunity to ask these questions.

Who is present in the boardroom eventually affects who is present in management, as the board decides who will be a company's next CEO and corporate officers. (Studies have shown that having three or more women in management is a business imperative – opening up a new pipeline of talent, improving corporate image, and resulting in higher company ratings on organizational dimensions, including work environment, leadership, accountability, and innovation.[14])

---

[12] Devillard, Sandrine, McKinsey & Company, *Women Matter*, 10 (2007), available at http://www.mckinsey.com/careers/women/makingadifference/socialsectorimpact/womenmatter/.

[13] *2006 Catalyst Census of Women Board Directors* (www.catalyst.org).

[14] Devillard, Sandrine, McKinsey & Company, *Women Matter*, (2007), available at http://www.mckinsey.com/careers/women/makingadifference/socialsectorimpact/womenmatter/.

Even as an investor, or potential investor, you can gather a significant amount of information about who is in the board-room of various companies and advance gender diversity as a priority. Some investors have pursued "socially responsible investing," by working with funds such as the Calvert Group, Ltd. Calvert defines socially responsible investing as allowing shareholders to "align their investment [portfolios] with their personal values by avoiding companies that do not meet certain standards."[15] Calvert researches companies, presents this research front and center on its website, and, in addition to being an active shareholder (filing nearly forty resolutions related to board diversity in ten years), rates companies' social responsibility.

Other investment funds, such as TIAA-CREF, the Council of Institutional Investors, and California Public Employees' Retirement System (CalPERS) "all reference board diversity in their corporate governance guidelines" as best practices.[16] Consider which funds you hold a stake in, and how you can encourage them to begin or continue practices to encourage socially responsible behavior by the companies *they* invest in.

It really does matter who is in a company's boardroom, and each of you has the opportunity, through your research and inquisitiveness, to make the topic of boardroom diversity a priority for many companies.

---

[15] Calvert Group, Ltd., available at www.calvert.com/sri.html (last visited December 17, 2007).

[16] Denise Nappier, *Bringing Diversity to the Boardroom: Connecticut's Unique Partnership*, available at www.state.ct.us/ott/articles/Article030103.pdf (last visited September 27, 2007).

CLOSING REMARKS

Women who have a passion for business should consider their goals for both vertical and Horizontal Advancement™. In this book, I have shared with you some best practices for achieving success in both areas.

I hope this information helps you achieve the success you are seeking.

Lynn Shapiro Snyder

January 2008

ABOUT THE PUBLISHER

Women Business Leaders of the U.S. Health Care Industry Foundation™

The WBL Foundation is a non-profit organization exclusively dedicated to senior executive women and women board members who work in or with the U.S. health care and life sciences industry. Unlike trade associations or other women's organizations, WBL provides a forum for senior executive women and women board members in the health care industry to network exclusively with other senior executive women from across all segments of the U.S. health care and life sciences industry. This includes manufacturers, payers, providers, and service providers to the U.S. health care and life sciences industry. To date, more than 1,700 senior executive women and women board members currently participate in WBL. WBL's Foundation Associates participate by invitation only. WBL relies on its annual Summit and various sponsorships to fund year long activities.

WBL's Mission Statement

The mission of the WBL Foundation is to help senior executive women and women board members in the health care industry improve their businesses and continue to grow professionally. The WBL Foundation achieves that mission by working to:

✦ facilitate networking opportunities for senior executive women and women board members in the health care industry,

✦ increase the visibility of senior executive women and women board members in the health care industry,

✦ expand the number of senior executive women in the health care industry, and

✦ increase the number of senior executive women from the health care industry who serve as members of boards of directors.

For more information, visit www.womenleadinghealthcare.org.

ABOUT THE AUTHOR

Lynn Shapiro Snyder, Esq.

Founder and President
Women Business Leaders of the
U.S. Health Care Industry Foundation,
and Senior Member,
Epstein Becker & Green, P.C.

1227 25th Street, NW, Suite 700
Washington, D.C. 20037

Phone: (202) 861-1806
Fax: (202) 296-2882

LSnyder@ebglaw.com

Lynn Shapiro Snyder is the Founder and President of the Women Business Leaders of the U.S. Health Care Industry Foundation ("WBL Foundation"). See www.womenleadinghealthcare.org. Ms. Snyder founded this 501 (c) (3) non profit organization in 2001, with founding sponsor Epstein Becker & Green, P.C., in order to meet the unmet needs of senior executive women in the U.S. health care industry. The mission of the Foundation is to help senior executive women in the health care industry improve their businesses and continue to grow professionally, through increased networking opportunities and by expanding the number of these senior executive women who serve as a member of a board of directors.

Through Ms. Snyder's efforts, the Foundation has held several successful Summits (the Foundation's major annual network-ing event), and Ms. Snyder has grown the Foundation from a select group of 40 to include a network of over 1,700 senior executive women and women board members—both in the United States and abroad—who do business with the U.S. health care and life sciences industry. In addition, Ms. Snyder and the WBL Foundation have assisted with many board searches, successfully having WBL Foundation Associates placed on these boards of directors, both for profit and non-profit.

Her efforts to foster "Horizontal Advancement™" of these senior executive women have made Ms. Snyder a nationally recognized speaker on the topics of corporate governance and gender diversity in the boardroom. In addition to authoring this book, Snyder is co-author of three editions of <u>Answering the Call: Understanding the Duties, Risks & Rewards of Corporate Governance</u>, a book for men and women considering board service. Thousands of copies of <u>Answering the Call</u> have been distributed to executives in many different industries.

Ms. Snyder's role as Founder of the WBL Foundation has earned her national media attention. In 2007, she was named a "Woman to Watch" by Jewish Women International. In April 2005, *Modern Healthcare* magazine named Ms. Snyder as one of the "Top 25 Women in Healthcare." In August 2002, *Modern Healthcare* magazine named Ms. Snyder as one of the "100 Most Powerful People in Healthcare" in its inaugural list.

In addition to founding the WBL Foundation, Ms. Snyder is a senior member of the law firm, Epstein Becker & Green, P.C. Ms. Snyder serves on the firm's Board. The law firm has one of the largest health care and life sciences practices in the United States. Ms. Snyder has almost thirty years of experience at the firm advising clients about federal, state, and international health law issues, including Medicare, Medicaid, TriCare, com-pliance, and managed care issues. She chairs the Third Party Payment Group and co-chairs the Health Care Fraud Practice Group. Her clients include health care providers, payors, phar-maceutical/device manufacturers, and those companies and financial services firms that support the health care and life sciences industry. She is a frequent speaker and publishes extensively. In the May 2006 issue of *Nightingale's Healthcare News*, Ms. Snyder was named one of the "Outstanding Fraud & Compliance Lawyers for 2006." In both the 2006 and 2007 editions of *The Best Lawyers in America*, Ms. Snyder was listed in the specialty of Health Care Law. She also has been quoted in the *New York Times* and other leading publications. Ms. Snyder's experience includes:

✦ Serving as lead defense counsel for several health care firms, including one of the largest pharmaceutical firms, one of the largest home health service firms, and one of the largest respiratory services firms in connection with significant fraud investigations/settlements with the federal and state governments;

✦ Representing several private equity investment banking firms regarding health regulatory compliance issues for large health care firm transactions including lead health regulatory counsel for the buyout of HCA by three private equity firms;

✦ Previously serving as outside General Counsel for over a decade to the American Managed Care and Review Association, one of the national trade associations for HMOs, PPOs, and UROs.

With respect to Ms. Snyder's international law activities, she has attended five health care business missions—Belgium 1995, Israel 1997, Brazil 1999, Italy 2002, Argentina 2005 and the Czech Republic 2006. She visited Israel in 2007 on a WBL Foundation business mission. She was board recertified as a Specialist in Health Law in the State of Florida for the period August 1, 2003-July 31, 2008.

Ms. Snyder represented several health trade associations during the enactment of the 1977 Medicare Anti-Fraud and Abuse Amendments and the 1978 HMO Amendments. Ms. Snyder has served as a member of: (1) the State of Florida Agency for Health Care Administration Health Care Fraud and Abuse Working Group (1993-1994); and (2) the Study Panel on Reforming the Fee-for-Service Medicare Program, sponsored by the National Academy of Social Insurance (1996-1998).

Ms. Snyder joined Epstein Becker & Green in 1979 and is admitted to practice law in the District of Columbia, the State of Florida, and before the United States Supreme Court. She earned a B.A. in Economics from Franklin & Marshall College in 1976 and her J.D. from the George Washington University National Law Center in 1979. On a more personal note, Ms. Snyder is married to Jeffrey M. Snyder and has three children, Rachel, Isaac, and Eitan. She works in the Washington, D.C. office.

See www.ebglaw.com for additional information about the law firm and for a more detailed biography of Lynn Shapiro Snyder.

Current and Former Board Positions:

Board member, Founder, Women Business Leaders of the U.S. Health Care Industry Foundation

Board member, Trustmark Mutual Holding Company

Board member, Maryland Israel Development Center

Board member, Epstein Becker & Green, P.C.

Advisory Board, Washington Institute for Israel Health Policy Research

Advisory Board, Academy for International Health Studies

Advisory Board, BNA Health Care Fraud Reporter

Advisory Board, Protocare Sciences

Education:

J.D., George Washington University National Law Center, 1979

B.A., Franklin & Marshall College, 1976, Phi Beta Kappa, Magna Cum Laude, Major: Economics/Health Economics

Memberships:

American Bar Association, Health Care White Collar Crime Committee

American Health Lawyers Association

Benjamin Rush Society, Franklin & Marshall College, Advisory Council

Health on Wednesday, a group of Women Health Policy Experts, Founding Member

Women Business Leaders of the U.S. Health Care Industry Foundation

WOMEN BUSINESS LEADERS
OF THE
U.S. HEALTH CARE INDUSTRY FOUNDATION™

WWW.WOMENLEADINGHEALTHCARE.ORG

PROMOTING HORIZONTAL ADVANCEMENT™

ORDER FORM
Advancing Women in Business:
10 BEST PRACTICES
with a special focus on board placement
By Lynn Shapiro Snyder

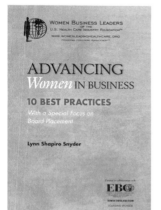

At the Inaugural WBL Summit in 2002, a group of about eighty senior executive women from the health care industry met in small groups to discuss their careers and their career advancement (both vertical and horizontal advancement™). These women collectively identified their most important wisdom and advice that they would give to other women looking to advance in business. This collective wisdom was used to form WBL's "Ten Best Practices for Advancing Women in Business." All proceeds from this book benefit WBL.

This book explores various ways to approach each of these ten best practices – with examples and action items. The book also examines ten best practices for making the board nominating committee's "radar screen" in order to gain corporate board seats – one of the core principles of horizontal advancement.™

$19.95 per book, plus shipping

Advancing Women in Business – Order Form

Your Name: _____

Your Title: _____

Your Company: _____

"Ship-to" Name & Address: _____

Your Phone Number: _____

Number of Copies & Total Amount: _____

Pay by sending this form to WBL via fax at (202) 861-3531 or email to WBL at ssadowski@ebglaw.com. For pre-sale, you may pay by credit card only; WBL accepts Visa, MasterCard, and American Express, and your card will not be charged until the book is ready to be shipped. Any questions, contact WBL at (202) 955-7181. Please complete the following:

Name as it appears on Credit Card: _____

Credit Card Number: _____

Expiration Date: _____

Signature: _____

AWB1

WOMEN BUSINESS LEADERS
OF THE
U.S. HEALTH CARE INDUSTRY FOUNDATION™

WWW.WOMENLEADINGHEALTHCARE.ORG
PROMOTING *HORIZONTAL ADVANCEMENT™*

ORDER FORM
Answering the Call:

Understanding the Duties, Risks, and Rewards of Corporate Governance
By Lynn Shapiro Snyder, Esq. and Robert D. Reif, Esq.

This book provides an overview of what one should consider as a member of a board of directors–including an overview of the various areas where a director may be held personally liable, what it means to be qualified for an audit committee, best practices for good corporate governance, and an in-depth look at D&O insurance written by the experts – representatives from a D&O insurance firm. All proceeds from this book benefit WBL.

This book also explores the benefits of gender diversity in the boardroom, in an effort to help men and women "Answer the Call" for board service.

- 1 book: $24.95 per book plus shipping
- 2-12 books: $21.95 per book plus shipping* (a "Board set")
- 13 books or more: $19.95 per book plus shipping*

Books also can be purchased at www.womenleadinghealthcare.org

---

Answering the Call: Third Edition – Order Form

Your Name: _____

Your Title: _____

Your Company: _____

"Ship-to" Name & Address: _____

Your Phone Number: _____

Number of Copies & Total Amount: _____

Pay by sending this form to WBL via fax at (202) 861-3531 or email to WBL at ssadowski@ebglaw.com. You may pay by credit card only; WBL accepts Visa, MasterCard, and American Express, and your card will not be charged until the book is ready to be shipped. Any questions, contact WBL at (202) 955-7181. Please complete the following:

Name as it appears on Credit Card: _____

Credit Card Number: _____

Expiration Date: _____

Signature: _____

* For discount to be applicable, books must be bought simultaneously.

AWB1